Dear Fear Teen

Powerful Stories By Extraordinary Teens On Living Your Best Life On The Other Side Of Fear

P2P Branded

Professional Photography:

Phase One Photography

Book Coaching:

Tiana Patrice

This book is intended to push you from the place that fear is attempting to keep you bound. This book is intended to give you hope and position you for purpose. This book is not intended to provide financial, health or legal advice. Please seek the appropriate counsel for financial, health or legal matters.

*Thank You To All Of The Families
For Allowing Your Children To Share Their Stories
& Their Voices To Be Heard...*

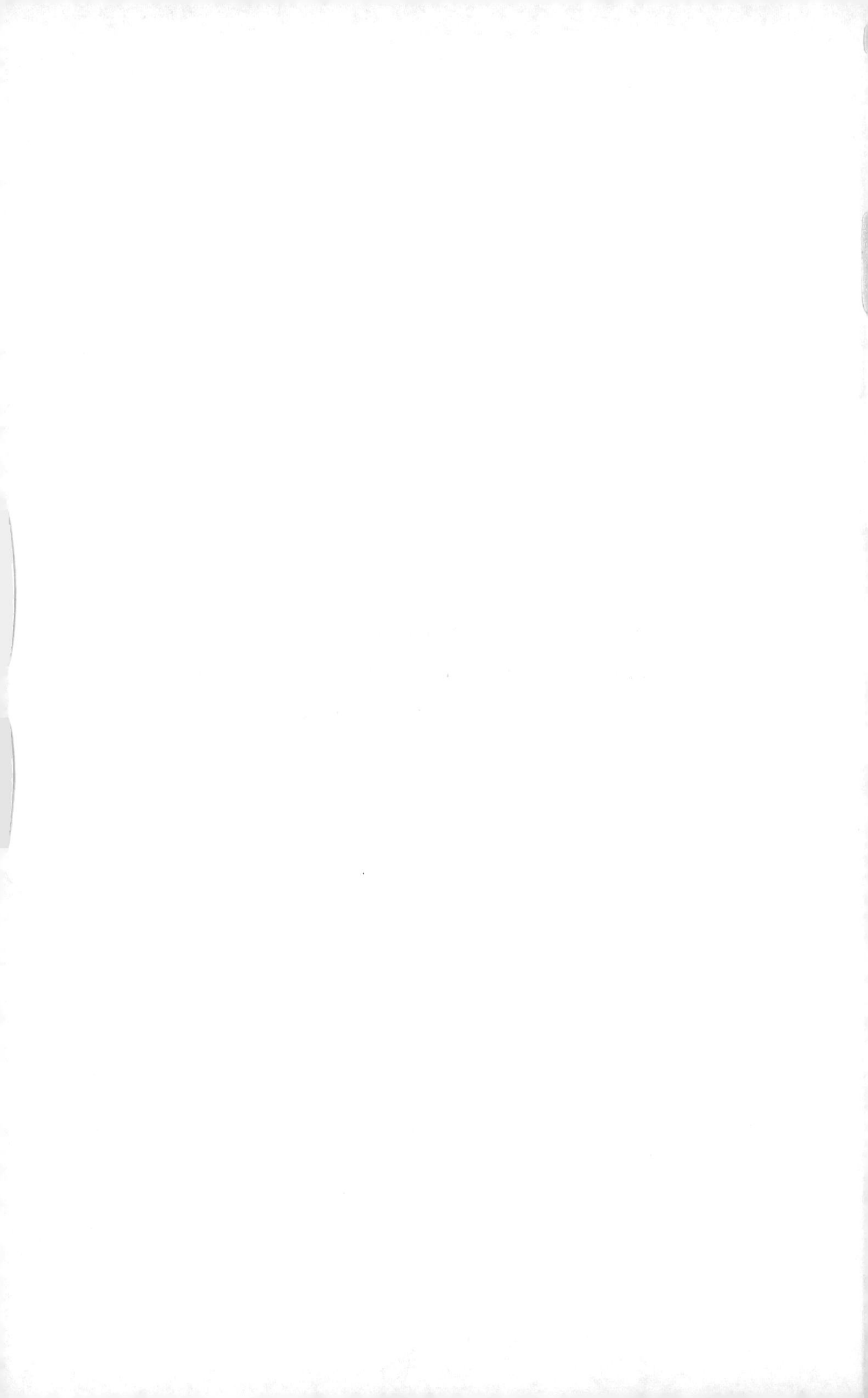

Contents

About The Visionary Author

Tiana Patrice is wife, mother of 3 and child of God. She is a 3 time best selling author, award-winning global speaker, executive coach and the founder of Women's CEO Alliance, a Coworking and consulting company designed to take businesses to the next level. To date, Tiana has launched 2 Dear Fear Book Anthologies, and now Dear Fear Teen Volume 1. The third volume of Dear Fear is set to release Spring 2019. She conducts workshops for companies and organizations on being a Fearless Leader in life, career and business, and provides intentional business, branding and marketing strategies to executive leaders, corporations and business owners. She is a highly sought after speaker for industry and professional groups like Women's Economic Forum, Hyundai, and Peak Performers Institute, where she shared her message globally with more than 30,000 leaders. Other organizations for which she has shared her success tactics and expertise include: The Small Business Administration, Delta Sigma Theta, Dothan Area Chamber of Commerce, Troy State University, and many others. Her messages have been spotlighted in Forbes, Huffington Posts and on stations such as Good Morning Washington, NBC, ABC and CBS. She is indeed the one to call if you are tired of letting fear hold you back in life, career and in business. Hailed as The Fearless Activator by her peers, Tiana helps her audience realize their fullest potential, let go of self-limiting beliefs, divorce their comfort zone and take immediate action on the other side of fear. For speaking inquiries, email info@tianapatrice.com. For more information on Women's CEO Alliance, head to www.womensceoalliance.com.

A Message From The Visionary Author

I'm so grateful that you are deciding to embark on this exciting journey of activating your fearLESS and beginning to live your best life on the other side of fear. I know what it feels like to be plagued by feelings of defeat, overwhelm and self-sabotaging thoughts. I know what it feels like to lose friends and feel as if you have no one to talk to. I know what it feels like to be your own worst critic.

I get it.

Fear tries to come in and convince us that we aren't worthy or not enough. Fear tries to tell us that we don't matter and aren't valuable. Fear tries to take our future and our dreams. **But fear can not and will not win!**

In this book, Dear Fear Teen, we have pulled together 5 brilliant teens telling their stories of how fear attempted to keep them shackled in fear, unhappiness, and inadequacy, but how God pulled them out. They are courageously sharing their truths with you in an effort to help you find your voice and share your truth too. If you ask them, they will tell you that this journey hasn't been easy. But it's been liberating and rewarding, and for many, provided healing and deliverance.

As you take this journey, dive into each chapter and use the tools in the book. This is the season for you to lean into who you are, push through fear, and hear what God is saying about you. I'm excited for you to take this journey with us. I'm excited about what's to come for you and the release you will feel from writing in the pages of this book. This is just the beginning. It has begun.

With Love,
Tiana Patrice
Visionary Author

How To Use This Book

This book is meant to be more than just read. It is meant to transform your way of thinking, inspire you to dream bigger than you've ever dreamt, and give you the tools to take immediate action against your fear. The stories inside are those of courage and resilience, but most importantly the transparency of the authors will leave you encouraged to share your story too.

You will find questions at the end of each chapter inside the pages of Dear Fear Teen. Be sure to answer each question, as they will guide you to more clarity in your life.

The strategically designed pages give you access to color your imagination with the positive affirmation coloring pages. This book will give you the tools to take immediate action against YOUR fear.

In the back of the book you will find pages for you to journal and share your story. It's important that you have a place to store your thoughts, as well as someone positive to talk to.

We are here to declare with you that you are **BOLD**. You are **ROYAL**. You are **DESERVING**. You are **EXCELLENT**. And fear has no more power over your life.

We are on a mission to liberate teens and women from the fear attempting to rob them of their destiny. Join the movement at www.amillionfearlessstrong.org.

Tayler
Somerville

Dear Fear,

You have made me worry and stress. You have continuously made me wonder if I was good enough. All my childhood you have led me down dark and depressing paths; as a 10-year-old, a 13-year-old and even at 16. You have persuaded me to believe that I am less than I am.

You have led me to underestimate myself. You disguise yourself as a friend that is trying to help me rather than hurt me. That will go on no longer. I am pushing you away. I am ignoring you, belittling you, and I am unfriending you. You will no longer push me down and prevent me from living out my youth the way I want to. You have always told me how to live, but now I am taking control. I will live my life the way I was designed to. You cannot and will not stop me because I know I am good enough. I will no longer allow the fear of judgement to take over my life. I am powerful, and I know God will always have me. Although you are a part of my story, you do not define it.

Signed,

Tayler Somerville

Dear Fear, You Can't Have My Youth

Have you ever lost yourself? I mean, have you really lost the essence of what really made you...you? I bet you'd never think that a 12-year-old could be having this conversation. Or that a 12-year-old could experience anxiety 24/7, right? But this one did. At the ripe ol' age of 12, I began to lose myself. Keep reading and I'll tell you why.

Typically, I am a sensitive, goofy, yet complicated person. When I was younger, I stressed a lot and it only got worse as I got older. I'm unsure where this came from, but it's my truth. I always felt different from the other kids, and I never felt cool enough to play with them. I felt like they singled me out because I dressed different and I was taller than most of my class.

To be honest, the people that were nice to me felt bad for me. That's a horrible way to make friends, by the way.

I convinced myself that as time went on, as we became older and moved into higher grades, things would change. Boy, was I wrong! When I got to middle school the bomb went off. I was surrounded by so many different kids and so many personalities that I completely lost who I was. I was stuck in a world where I didn't know who I was and what my purpose was. I looked all around and saw smiling faces on everyone else, but I couldn't find mine. I missed Tayler Marie, the goofy girl I used to be. I could not pinpoint the source of my sadness. In this season, I began to hate who I was because fear told me I was different and no one liked me for me. Every time I attempted to shake the voice of fear, it whispered over my shoulder, again and again, that I was not good enough.

For years I allowed this sadness to consume me, and I hid all behind a smile. I didn't talk to anyone about it. Just thinking about what people would think, and how they'd treat me from then on, made me nervous. I didn't want to go out, I didn't want to hold conversations, and I didn't want to hang out with friends very often. Most of my time in middle school was spent with a lack of self-worth and pain. As I write this, I realize that many of my peers were experiencing the same thing and afraid to speak out. One day I looked up and realized that I had allowed the fear of being judged by others to consume my life. I was living, but not *living*. Does that make sense? I was wasting my youth.

Girl, I felt so alone. I felt like there was no one there for me, you know? Now may I remind you, I was only 12 and 13. For years, I still felt useless. Fear told me, "Oh c'mon! Do you really think they want you here? You are better off home alone." And that is exactly what I did.

In January of 2017, I cut most of my hair off. I did this because I wanted to let go of who I used to be. I wanted to let go of my past. It was my way of coming out of the closet that fear had pushed me into. I was left between ½ inch and 1 inch of hair on my head. I felt freer and more confident. I felt like me again! I was ready to knock fear off my shoulder. But a few months later, I started high school.

My first year of high school, fear found its way back into my life. I became very anxious again, all the time. I was confused and overwhelmed. Months later, I had my first panic attack. It was a horrifying and uncomfortable experience. I was at volleyball practice when it happened. I used to get so nervous at practice and tournaments because fear told me I was no good. I was so afraid to mess up and play badly that I didn't even get to enjoy that season. My parents didn't understand when I told them what happened. I understand that now because I never told them what was going on. My line has always been, "I'm fine." What does "I'm fine" mean? Saying "I'm fine" just means you are too scared to express how you feel. Maybe fear is convincing you that no one cares about how you feel or your emotions are just too much. The reality is I wasn't fine, and I had to open up and talk to someone about it. I had to pick myself up, dust myself off. I had to say three words that helped change my life, "I'm not ok."

The fear of being judged kept me from speaking out. It silenced my voice. But now I'm not afraid to share my truth. I know it will help someone. Fear filled the past few years of my life with sadness and hurt. I felt broken, but fear will not take my future. Every day, by the grace of God, I am healing. In Him, I find my strength. I know that I don't have to be afraid to admit where I am weak because that's when God is strong.

Girl, please do not let fear do the same to you. Do not let it take over your life and your youth. You should be going out, hanging out with friends and family, having fun, learning and growing. You can't do those things with fear hanging on your shoulder. Overcoming the fear of judgment and lack of self-worth isn't easy, but it is so important.

I may be young, but I've learned you must believe in yourself and the power God has given you. Don't be afraid to make changes in your life. Go pray, go meditate. Have an at-home spa day, go see the movie you wanted to see. Exercise and spend time with the people you love. Take care of **you**.

If no one has told you today, I want you to know that you are enough. You are more than enough. Do not waste your time and your life being afraid of the opinions of others. Honestly, their opinions don't matter. If they do not appreciate you for who you are, they don't deserve your time or your friendship. Don't allow fear to take away from your life and keep you from living. Loving and believing in yourself opens a door of light and a path leading to success andjoy. Block out bad energy and bad vibes and just allow yourself to be you, be free, and be young. And declare with me...Dear Fear, You Can't Have My Youth!

Questions:

When was a time the fear of judgement took over your life?

____

____

____

What is one way you will take back your youth?

____

____

____

Tayler Somerville

Chapter Wrap Up

Have you ever been stuck in a place of not feeling good enough? In this story, Tayler shares with us how the negative side of "enough" can sneak in and rob you of happiness, joy, and truly living your best life. Fear uses this tactic of "enough" to convince you that you aren't worthy of making good grades, you aren't deserving of making the basketball team, or you're not pretty enough to enter that pageant. These thoughts are the furthest thing from the truth!

You are enough, you are deserving, you are beautiful and brilliant! Don't allow fear to infiltrate your mind and tell you otherwise. Fear has a job to do, and that is to keep you from being awesome. Don't allow fear to win.

My favorite part of Tayler's chapter was when she said, "Believe in yourself and the power God has given you." Always remember that God gave you power to overcome anything you are going through, but He did NOT give you the spirit of Fear!

Today, make the decision to change your mind and begin to think of enough as the best thing that has happened to you. When fear says, "You aren't enough," you say, **"I AM MORE THAN ENOUGH."** Allow God to turn what fear meant for bad into something so awesome and good for you!

I AM
FEARLESS

Kala
Inman

Dear Fear,

Fear, you do exist, but you cannot control what I do anymore. In middle school you told me I wasn't good enough. You led me to believe hiding myself was a good option. If I hid myself, no one would see me. You made me feel as if my 4C hair wasn't pretty enough. You made me feel bad about the unknown parts of my family, and told me the only way to get over that was to keep it to myself. Fear, you told me to compare my life to others just to point out that I was not them. But fear, you are not allowed to hold me back from my full potential anymore. I will have a good relationship with my natural self. I do belong. I will enjoy life. Fear, you kept me from being myself physically and emotionally. But no more. Fear you have to go! I will no longer be afraid of talking and expressing myself.

Signed,

Kala Inman

Dear Fear You Can't Hide Me

"Oh it's about that time, ain't it?"
"You'd look better with it straight."
"I liked it the other way!"

Growing up, I never liked conflict. I was always the one to engage with people in a peaceful presence, although I didn't have peace inside. Can you relate? My name is Kala. I grew up the only child in a home occupied by three. When I was younger, I always gave to others, did what I was asked and tried not to cause fuss or disappointment to anyone. I never liked conflict, and I avoided it at all costs. Because of this I rarely talked to others, and I certainly never talked about myself...including my feelings.

I remember a time during my middle school years when I did not like my hair relaxed anymore. The chemicals were too strong for my hair and caused major damage and breakage to my strands. In fact, the summer before my seventh grade year I had to get a haircut. Being so young, it felt like painful surgery to my image. The sides were cut to my ear, the front just below my eyebrows, and the back shaved down. I had to get this haircut because the unrelaxed portion of my hair in the back broke off the relaxed portions. One of the last times I had gotten a relaxer, it burned too much, and the other side did not get enough time to process. There were mornings I would take down my head wrap and one side of my head was harder to comb and looked different than the rest. Sadly, the haircut was inevitable, and it was awful for me. I did not want to go to school with it, but I did not have a choice. Summer was over. School supplies were back on the shelves, and I was back walking the halls. This time I was on a journey of natural hair that I wasn't quite ready for.

As my hair grew, I noticed that the back of my hair, which was once shaved, was growing out with a kink. This baffled me, as I didn't have the acceptable curls and waves everyone loves. Where were my curls? Nowhere to be found. To sum it up, my hair was what you call nappy, and people around me made sure that I knew it. While I was happy to see it was growing, I soon realized that my growth came at a cost. A cost that my confidence ended up paying. I felt incomplete because it was not a process I had wanted to go through, but I had no choice. Can you relate with having to go through something, even when you didn't want to?

However, I learned that I had to embrace the process and learn to love the journey.

In order for my hair to grow in sync, I had to make the ultimate choice and get the "big chop". The treatment I got was horrible. People made jokes and rude comments behind my back. Friends turned their back on me. They stared, pointed and laughed. It was the worst experience ever. For everyone middle school is tough. For me, a 4C hair textured female, it was so much worse. My confidence was racking up a big bill, and my account was overdrawn. Fear began to set in and told me, "You should only do what people like. Nobody likes it, so change it."

Fear discouraged me, I was in an emotional bind. I could have just relaxed my hair and it would have been over, but that means fear would have won. And I would have lost my power to nonsense. There were times I would be so angry I'd want to fight. But that wasn't my personality. Altercations and conflict aren't who I am. I knew something had to change. I had to find a way to get my confidence back. Instead of relaxing or straightening my hair, I learned more about natural products and I applied the best ones for my hair type. I learned how to style my hair and keep it healthy. That healthy state included no chemical processing, heatless styling, and plenty of moisture. I learned how to not only transition into my natural hair, but also transition out of hate. An easy word to say, but a hard emotion to get rid of. But I did it. I turned hate into love.

In my seventh grade year, I had a math teacher that came to me personally. She and another teacher said they liked my hair, with the other stating she had friends that went natural and liked their style. My confidence account was back overflowing and it was attracting others to own their confident selves too.

When I decided to go natural, I wondered why no one really understood my journey. I wondered why it was such an issue, and I started to doubt my adjustments. I realized that self expression is important and no one should take that away from you. Trying something new taught me not to be afraid to embrace my natural self. Now, I am 18. I'm a freshman in college, living my life and encouraging others to make sure they appreciate themselves for who they are. I feel I have come a long way in life. I have dealt with unfair treatment from peers about appearances, but never stopped doing what I thought was right for myself!

I will encourage you, as a reader, to never let yourself be displaced from your personal beliefs. And if that's your hair, don't feel ashamed of your texture of hair. Embrace it and keep it healthy. Always know that the hate you receive will only be temporary, and people that think the worst of you are not for you. And you will just have to be ok with that.

Questions:

Has there been a time in your life when you felt uncomfortable about who you are?

____

____

____

What are some positive things you can do to help increase your confidence?

____

____

____

Kala Inman

Chapter Wrap Up

Have you ever gone through an uncomfortable process? Maybe it was cutting your hair, or a new journey of making better choices in life. In this chapter, Kala shared with us how processes can be super uncomfortable and hard. Going through a process isn't always easy, but positive processes are absolutely necessary. Sometimes people won't get you or understand.

There may even be times people turn away. This doesn't mean anything is wrong with you, nor does it mean to stop the process. This means you should trust the process and embrace it. Even when it's hard, your process has a purpose. Think about it. Was there something you learned at the end of your process? Did you learn something new about yourself? Is there something you can now teach others? If you answered yes, then your process had a purpose! I know it may not sound easy now, but trust me, you'll understand more and more as the process continues.

The process is designed to position you for greater things. Many times your process is much bigger than you. It's meant for you to help someone else, just as Kala did in this chapter. While she was in the process, it seemed unbearable, but at the end of it all she found her voice and her confidence. Because of this, she encouraged other people to embrace their hair and find their confidence too. In this season, I encourage you to take a deep breath and declare victory over your process. You are Not Defeated. You are Victorious. In Jesus Name!

I AM
UNIQUE

Heather
De'Amario

Dear Fear,

You have made me cower down and let people walk all over and mistreat me. You have caused so many people I loved to break me. You have watched me curl into a ball and break down every morning and night for six months. You have made me feel like such a pariah that I can no longer go out in public without feeling immense anxiety. You have bullied me, abused me, and nearly killed me. For 8 years, you have tormented me.

You have tormented me to the point that I put a glass wall up and faked being tough so I could make myself and others believe that I can't be hurt. However, we all know what happens when some people see valuables behind a glass window. They throw rocks at the glass to shatter the walls and break them down. Fear, you have done this to me over and over again.

I have decided that from this point on, I will use fear as a learning experience. As much of an enemy fear has been to me, it has also been one of the greatest teachers I have ever encountered, as it has taught me the importance of self-worth and confidence.

I have learned that no matter what, I need to be unapologetically me. Life is too short to be pointing out insecurities about yourself that others may not notice. Having said that, life is also too short to let others tear you down and point out attributes of your appearance or personality to make you feel small and insecure. I think it's time that I learn one of the greatest lessons fear has taught me so far, which is to love myself.

Signed,

Heather De'Amario

Dear Fear You Can't Have My Identity

From the ages of 3 to 8 I lived in Lindenhurst, Long Island. Growing up in Lindenhurst seemed as if I was living in a dollhouse. On the surface it seemed as if everyone had that perfect Barbie and Ken relationship. A relationship in which couples rarely fight. A relationship where both partners were madly in love and were planning on growing old together. Whenever you would see them they'd be laughing, holding hands, giving that stereotypical "lovey dovey" smile. As it turns out, they were just much better at hiding their truth than my parents were.

Although our home looked beautiful outside, green grass, barbed fence, garden strip with beautiful flowers planted by our landlord, inside our house felt like a warzone. My parents would constantly argue. For me, this was normal, especially when I noticed that my home wasn't the only one with issues.

I remember when my mother and I moved in with my father after living with my uncle.

This was a happy moment for me knowing that I would be living with both my parents. I thought it would be nice to feel like a normal complete family. A family with two parents who loved each other and lived in one of those, "too good to be true" suburban neighborhoods. It took me a few years to realize that living with both of my parents wasn't all it was cut out to be. As often I could remember my father's anger issues were so extreme that it affected his job status. He made financial decision without my mom that often left us without food and other things we needed in our home.

Almost every night there was an argument. Usually, the arguments started with my mom asking my dad if he could calm down on the eating out and the careless spending. Then everything would just go 0 to 100. All I can remember was hearing my father call my mother derogatory names and say degrading words to her, words I **cannot** repeat. My mom would then retaliate and say rude things to him. It was a nightmare.

When my parents argued, I would sit in my room and build Legos and play with dolls or curl into a ball and pray that God would just end my life then and there. I didn't really want that to happen, but for some reason I thought the only way to be free from it all was for God to take me away. There are some prayers God doesn't answer. I'm so glad that was one of them. When my parents would argue I learned to mediate and distract them with comedy. This unhealthy habit to cover up pain with laughter and enjoy the attention I received, also translated into my social life at school.

My sense of humor and love of attention caused me to grow up being fairly confident.

Even though people would call me weird because I didn't fit the mold for a young girl in Lindenhurst. That girl was a cheerleader with long blonde hair who wore Uggs, shorts, and Pink tee-shirts. That wasn't me. I took pride in being different. I was my own beautiful and funny person. I was never ashamed of who I was. This isn't to say the teasing didn't hurt, it did, but I didn't allow it to shake my confidence and happiness. I knew my identity and I **thought** no one could take that from me.

When I was eight, my parents and I moved to Hunters Creek, Florida. My mom began her third year as a teacher and my dad was beginning his fourth year a driver. Having my father as a limo driver was actually kind of cool. There were times my dad had early shifts, and he would take me to school in a black stretch and everyone would stare at me. I felt famous.

Although it seemed cool, my mother knew that inevitably she would have to make some big decisions. She put me in therapy soon after moving to Florida so that I would have someone to talk to before my parents divorce. After the divorce my father blamed me. He told me that it was my fault our family wasn't the same. He would say things such as "Are you happy now" and "How can you live with yourself?. He was breaking my sanity, and he didn't even care.

The Transfer

As if the divorce wasn't enough, after fourth grade I transferred schools and was now going to a charter school. I made two main friends in fifth grade. One of the friend's was fairly popular and had introduced me to a group of girls she had classes with. She and I would sit with them on occasion, however I would just fade into the background, peeping into the light of the conversations they'd have. Every now and then I would give a short reply as a reminder that I was still there.

In sixth grade, all of those girls were now in all of my classes. Within a week they had gotten significantly closer to my former best friend which pushed me to feel as if I needed to make a friendship with them. I found an opportunity to do so when it became news that the girls were going to the movies one weekend. They had planned all the logistics out in front of me which in my head meant that I was invited. Upon asking one of the girls to make sure I was invited, she chuckled and said that just because they planned it near me doesn't necessarily mean I was invited. I was so hurt. That entire week I was crying off and on.

Eventually, word that I wasn't invited had gotten to my former best friend. She felt so bad that she ended up inviting me so I wouldn't feel excluded. That night, only three girls out of the 11 people who were invited, tried to make me feel as if I belonged. The next day, someone posted a picture from that night on the group instagram. They tagged everyone in the picture, except for me, and captioned it, "squad". I commented asking why I wasn't tagged and whoever posted it said, "who said you were in the squad?". This was another reminder that despite how three of the people there made me feel, the majority never wanted me to show my face. I can tell you, there was no humor in this. And I did not like the attention this was bringing to me. My confidence was taking a hit.

From that point on, these girls made it a point to break me. They made fun of my appearance. They constantly belittled me. They told me I was ugly, that my feet were too long and I was never enough. They always attempted to label me as one race, which made me question my own identity. I felt as if everyone was always trying to take one of my races away from me. I felt alone and defeated. Those prayers to God from before slowly crept back in. Fear told me life wasn't worth living with this type of torment. Many nights I tried to rush God's timing. But there was one night, in an attempt of self sabotage, my phone received an alert to a live stream. It was Brendon Urie, and this live stream helped save my life.

Brandon talked about his anxiety and depression that he's faced and how he deals with it. It was nice to realize I wasn't alone. It was nice to know that someone else had experienced these things and learned how to deal with it. I thought I felt a twinkle of hope come back, however two days after the last day of school, the public sabotage came up again. This time, when the thoughts of self sabotage returned, I reached out to someone who cared and she talked me through it.

The Move

I moved to Maryland when I was 11 and going into 7th grade. I still hadn't shaken the feeling of not knowing who I was. I went from being this genuinely happy and energetic girl to being this really unhappy, empty, beaten down shell of myself. I went from identifying with every strand of my culture, and embracing my multiple backgrounds, to not knowing what I should identify as.

While I was separated from those old friends, I was not separated from the impact they had on me. I always felt vulnerable and empty, even in a new state. Fear that new friends would treat me the same. Fear that I wasn't enough. Fear that I'd never be enough for anyone. I had to learn about self-care in this season. As soon as I began taking care of myself and letting myself believe I was beautiful, I felt confident. It took me a while to truly be myself. To realize that no one can make me pick a side and an identity. To remember that me being bi-racial does not mean that I have to force myself to choose just one race to identify as. The truth is, if you know yourself, no one should be telling you who you are. We have to do a better job at knowing ourselves. I'm not going to lie, there are times that I still feel inadequate or empty. However, I have taught myself several ways for me to feel happier and I want to share that with you.

1. Spread joy and be nice to everyone. Be super sweet and welcoming.

2. With that said, don't think that being nice means that you have to allow people to walk over you. Always remember what others think doesn't define you.

3. Realize that it's ok to feel bad sometimes. You have a right to every emotion you feel. No one can tell you that your feelings aren't valid because no one knows your mind. It's just not ok to stay in that emotion. Rise up!

4. It's ok to have a core group of friends, but don't be cliquish. Open yourself up to new friendships and be open to being a new kind friend to someone else.

5. Realize that it's ok to take care of yourself and focus on you. Be your own priority. It doesn't make you selfish.

I guess what I'm saying is, know who you are and focus on your happiness. You're never alone. Share your story and your truth, and declare with me, Dear Fear, You Can't Take My Identity.

Heather De'Amario

Chapter Wrap Up

Have you ever felt broken? So broken that maybe you didn't know who you were? In Heather's chapter she shared that as her confidence began to shatter, she questioned who she was and her identity. Can you relate? It's easy to get lost in the sauce of life sometimes. It's easy to compare yourselves to others. It's easy to pretend like everything is ok when it's not. It's easy to smile when on the inside you want to scream. And because all of this is so easy, that's why it's easy to forget who we are.

However, even in those moments you must make a mindful decision to stop comparing yourself to others, you don't know their story or what they may have gone through. You must make the bold choice to get help when you need someone to talk to. You must own your power and only engage in friendships and relationships that are positive and respectful. Trust me there are friends out here that want to see you win! And lastly no matter what you are going through, harming yourself is never the answer.

Heather showed us the power of self-control and self-reflection within her story. She taught us that it's ok to reach out for help in our time of need. At the end of the chapter, Heather provided some great steps on how to transition yourself into the positive life you want to live in. Remember, no one can steal your power unless you decide to give it to them. Focus on being the best you that you can be!

I AM A CONQUEROR

Jamiya
Richardson

Dear Fear,

I see you think that it's a game over here, and you think it's a game you won! I don't understand why I let you control me! You took happiness from people all around me and not just the kids. My mom to be exact. This hurt me and thanks to you I thought I would have to carry this with me all my life. You let people enter my family's life knowing they weren't in it for the long run. You made me cry for days and nights thinking my mom would really get hurt. My mom loved that man, but you made me scared enough to where I was so mad every time I saw his face. I never would want my mom to be in that hurtful place again. You made her think she wasn't enough. You are the enemy of everyone. I don't think anyone should ever fall for you and your tricks. You know what Fear, I refuse to fall for them again, I will not let you hurt me! I will not blame myself for things that were meant to be, and I will do everything you wouldn't approve of. I will no longer cry and question GOD! And from now on, I'm in charge! And will live a Fearless life! Dear Fear, you can't take my Family!

Signed,

Jamiya Richardson

Dear Fear You Can't Have My Family!

Have you ever felt alone in the shadows? Well that was me at one point in my life. I almost felt deaf and could only hear the words Fear was telling me. My family was going through a situation, and I thought I would lose my Mom and other family members. Yes, at a very young age, my biggest fear wasn't falling from my bicycle. It was that my family would end. Everyday that went by, I could feel and see my Mom's pain. I watched my mom allow someone to hurt her over and over again and go right back to loving him like it never happened. She convinced herself that it was to keep her family together. But when I saw the marks and bruises, I asked myself, was it all worth it. When she hurt, I hurt. Those were the moments when I wanted to talk the most. But as a parent, she shut me out. She would always say she was a big girl and she could handle it. She would tell me to get out of the room while she was crying. I would get upset, not only did I want to be there for her, I needed her to be there for me. I felt alone. The shadows became my resting place. I hid my emotions and tears for fear of making things worse.

I couldn't talk to my little sister because she was little and only 5-years-old. She was just as upset as I was and would cry so hard. I had to protect her. And I did. I stayed strong. I brought my sister into the shadows with me. Now we both were silent and afraid.. My older cousin would let me talk to him, but he was in pain too. I was the grown-up for everyone at times. I knew my mom had to be a mom and a wife and I knew that put a lot of stress on her. Because of this, I had to put my focus into taking care of everyone else. I had nowhere to turn and Fear was the only one listening to me.

When my emotions became too much, I would find ways to escape and get away from Fear. I learned to write my feelings inside of a diary. I would go with my Nana because I felt safer with her and my Pop-Pop. Nana and Pop-Pop's house was where I felt free and was able to get away from it all. My sister and I would call Aunt Ty to see when she could come and get us. Instead of living a normal life, I was constantly searching for ways to escape my reality. I knew if we could spend a weekend with her, then we wouldn't have to deal with home.

One time, things at home got really bad. I remember fear trying to convince me that this was the last time I'd see my mom. It was the worst time of my life. I felt so helpless and alone. I went to school the next day, and instead of going to lunch I went to the counselor's office. Fear told me that my mom would get angry and leave me for telling her business. I didn't care anymore. I knew I needed to talk to someone, and to the counselor's office I went. I took my sister with me, because I wanted her to have someone to talk to as well. I would tell her how upset I was, and how I couldn't talk to my mom. I told her that I didn't understand why my mom would make this seem so normal. The counselor helped calm me and my sister down and gave us advice. She told me it was ok to give my Mom space and that she would be ok. She told me

Fear did not have to control me and this was a place where I could share my feelings. Fear could not find me in my secret places, but I would always have to go back home.

My grades began to drop. I was once an A student, and now was bringing home C's and D's. I couldn't focus in school, and I was always tired from staying up all night worried about my mom. Fear told me I was a disappointment to her for getting bad grades. Every day and night, I remember being scared and confused. What was going to happen? What was he going to do to my Mom? Was he going to come and get us too? Fear kept telling me he was coming for us next. I was upset, I couldn't stop crying. I felt alone, and my sister was too young to understand. I would race to lock our bedroom door and hold my little sister. Where was my Nana? Where were my aunts? Why would no one come and get us? Would I ever be safe in here? Sometimes I would just sit in the corner and write what I wanted to say. When my sister would cry and start shaking, I knew I had to be strong, so I would stop crying and just hold her. I would always pray they would break up. You wouldn't want your mom in an abusive relationship either. I believed in GOD and I know everything happens for a reason, but sometimes I wondered what the reason was. Why would GOD want me to watch my mom be upset and hurt?

God answered my prayers. My mom eventually left and we moved with my Nana & Pop-Pop. It was the best thing that ever happened to us. We were free again! Things started to change. I was able to start sleeping again. I paid better attention in class and landed back on Honor Roll all year. I am now closer to my Mom, and she encouraged me to share my truth and write my story.

In this chapter of my life, I learned that my voice matters and that it's ok to talk to someone. I also learned not to allow Fear to steal my voice. Not speaking up causes unnecessary stress and guilt. Fear may have had a piece of my story but not anymore. Fear tried to hold me back so much during this time. I was even afraid to release this chapter. I was afraid of what others would say, but my mom and Aunts encouragement helped me. I encourage you to step out of your comfort zone and let people know your story it could have a big impact on you in a good way. Dear Fear, You Can't Have My Family!

Questions

What is fear attempting to hold you back from?

____

____

____

What is something positive you can do to break through your fear?

____

____

____

Jamiya Richardson

Chapter Wrap Up

Have you ever felt as if you lost your voice? Have there been times you wanted to speak up but fear whispered in your ear that you wouldn't be heard? In Jamiya's chapter every time she wanted to share how she felt, fear told her that something bad would happen. Fear told her that her voice didn't matter. Fear told her that she wasn't valuable. That's what fear does. Can you relate? It creeps in and gives us the bad version of our own story, because it doesn't want us to know the truth.. How deceitful.

The truth is when you use your voice for good, great things happen. People are saved and set free. You are able to see that there is a greater life waiting for you on the other side of fear.

Fear has no right to your voice, because fear didn't give it to you. Don't allow fear to rob you of things that God gave to you.

If you are going through something and need an outlet, be like Jamiya, and find one in a close family member or counselor. You shouldn't have to go through anything alone. If you are struggling with finding your voice, understand that your voice matters! You matter. And fear can't take that away from you.

I AM
RESILIENT

Alaysha
Bell

Dear Fear,

Why am I still letting you control my life? I thought I was strong and an overcomer after all the challenges I have been through, but you are still here. You keep telling me I am not good enough and I will never be. You keep telling me that I am not worthy enough to receive all my blessings. But today, on August 11, 2018, I am acknowledging your presence and commanding you to move today. I will no longer allow you to take control of my mind, body, and soul. I thank you for coming into my life because without you I would not be who I am today. Who am I, you may ask? I am strong. I am beautiful. I am no longer afraid of you.

Signed,

Alaysha

Dear Fear, You Can't Have My Happiness

I never knew I was unhappy. I hid behind my big smile, pretending that everything was okay when it wasn't. I hid behind my smile because it helped me get through hardships and tribulations. My friends and family depended on me, so I couldn't be the unhappy one. Who wants to get help from someone who cannot even help herself?

For a long time, I had a bad habit of blocking individuals from my life who hurt me. I would rather act as if the person and all the pain they have caused didn't exist, than to express how I really felt. I did not want to address any heartbreak head on because it would make the outcome worse for me. Fear had me to assume that I would not be heard or understood, so what was the point? I self-evaluated all situations and circumstances from a place of fear and defeat, not realizing I was internalizing all my issues and problems.

The beginning of my internalization started at the age of seven: my parents' divorce.

When my parents divorced, my mother moved my siblings and I across the country to California, away from my father. Within less than a year, we headed back to Orlando, FL and resided there for an additional two and a half years. At this time, my relationship with my father was at its highest; I was the true definition of a daddy's girl. But not too far away, our relationship started to go downhill.

In 2010, my mother remarried and moved my siblings and I to Dade City, FL. Slowly, my relationship with my father deteriorated. I went from seeing my dad every two weeks, to once every four months, to no contact for a whole year. We barely communicated. There were occasional "check-up" texts, but no efforts from either side to rekindle the relationship. The move to Dade City was not the fault of our relationship, but it did play a major role in it.

I have been in Dade City for nearly a decade. I experienced puberty, graduated high school, and developed friendships and bonds with a lot of people in Dade City. I had no desire to go to my dad's because I was spending time with my friends. Honestly I was avoiding him because I was hurt.

My first and biggest heartbreak was from my father. By not being a present and an active participant in my life during my adolescent years, my father caused me the biggest disappointment of my life. When my father and mother was married, he was very present. Every Wednesday, he took my brother and I to the local library and Piccadilly's after school. I was grateful for that time with and it was a routine that I looked forward. I loved to read. I used to read five books within a week. But when the divorce happened, my love for reading didn't matter at all. All of the library trips stopped. It seemed as if my dad divorced both my mom and us.

I spent holidays and a few weeks during summer break with my father, but it was not the same. He was there, but he wasn't present. This was another reason why I did not desire going over to my dad's house a lot. Through high school, I rarely visited my dad. If he was not going to be "there", then there was no reason for me to be over there. I could be home with my cousins and friends.

Instead of going to him and expressing how I felt, I hindered him from entering in my life completely. I did not completely shut him out, but I did lack communication with him. If he called me, I would not answer. If he text me, I MAY text him back depending on my mood, but more than likely I did not. Our energies matched each others. Neither of us wanted to have the uncomfortable conversations. Because of our poor communication, he missed important moments in my life like seeing me go off to prom. Those little moment matter and will always be remembered with him not in it. Ultimately, me limiting my father's access in my life was only hurting me in the end. I was hurting myself by not speaking on it, FORGIVING, letting go, and moving forward.

It was not until the death of my great-grandfather that my father had a discussion about a few things (not everything, we still have more to discuss). Our communication improved slightly my senior year of high school and he was able to be a part of my ceremony for Outstanding Senior. The death of my grandfather put my perspective on relationships in a new light. Life is too short to dwell on the past and not move forward. One minute I am here, and the next minute I could be gone.

During this season, I learned that it is okay to not be okay. It is okay to be unhappy with certain situations or life at times. I just shouldn't stay stuck there. I must move forward. I learned that I block people out to protect myself, not realizing it is hurting me in the process. I knew what I wanted for the future, but my stubbornness stopped me from pushing forward because of my pain.

To be honest, right now, I am still struggling with internalization. But it's something I work on daily. It has both positive and negative effects on me. It gives me the ability to grow and understand myself before sharing with the world. I realize that I need time to be alone. However, suffering in silence can take over an individual's mind. No one can read my mind or understand my challenges if I am not expressing them. I have to continuously remind myself to not let a situation control my life because it is only temporary.

At this point in my life, as a young nineteen year old African American girl, I am a successful sophomore at the #1 Public Historical Black College/University, Florida Agricultural and Mechanical University. I am healthy, I am happy, and I am making the decision to move forward every single day. Dear Fear, You Can't Take My Happiness.

Alaysha Bell

Questions:

Have you ever been unhappy?

____

____

____

What can you do today to move forward and find your happiness again?

____

____

____

Alaysha Bell

Chapter Wrap Up

Have you ever been unhappy in life? Maybe you were just moving through the motions, but not truly embracing the joy inside of you. In Alaysha's chapter, she takes us on a journey of transition. As we know, many times in life, transition can be difficult and scary. But not impossible.

If you are going through a season in your life where you are unhappy, don't cover it up with unhealthy behaviors. That doesn't solve the problem. In fact it only creates new ones. The situation that you may be going through will only come together through self-reflection, prayer and forgiveness. Yes. The person that hurt you the most, you must forgive. Fear wants you to be angry and bitter. This is because fear doesn't want you to be free. When you are free, you are that much closer to your destiny.

Realize, forgiveness isn't for the next person to apologize to you. Forgiveness is for you. It's to release you from the bondage keeping you from your destiny. When you forgive genuinely you must simultaneously give up the right to hurt the person that hurt you. Forgiveness is a powerful tool of love, and self-reflecting allows you to see the areas in which you can improve in as well.

When Alaysha began to self-reflect, she realized that from her hurt, she put up a wall and blocked out her father. She realized that in order to fix the situation she too had work to do.

Good work. Positive work. Healing work. Don't be afraid of the work. The work will guide you into your next season. Take some time to self-reflect over your life and know that if you aren't where you want to be that's ok. Commit to making the change today that will take you into all that is waiting for you..

I AM
BEAUTIFUL

Dear Fear,

____

____

____

____

____

____

____

____

____

____

____

____

____

____

____

____

____

Signed,

____

Dear Fear Teen
Volume 1

Until Next Time. . .
www.dearfearbook.com

Journal Time